SMART MOVES

The Insiders Guide to
SUCCESSFUL CHANNEL PROMOTIONS

by Michelle Kabele

ISBN 978-0-9820686-5-6

Contents

Tune In

Getting your product from manufacturing to the end-user can send your goods flying along the express lane or down a long and winding road. You might be a manufacturer who goes direct to a consumer (business-to-consumer, or B2C). You might get to your customer via a channel partner (business-to-business, B2B), which actually makes this intermediary channel your customer as well, right?

In this more layered scenario, each channel in the process represents another customer. How do you motivate your channel partners to create demand from the next channel in line and drive those sales?

One of the answers is channel promotions.

Before we dive into this fascinating subject, let's just clarify the definition of "channel promotions" because there is some confusion out there. In this book, the term "channel promotions" refers to a promotional campaign that requires the participation of channel partners, meaning those associated businesses who help you sell your product or service, such as value-added resellers (VARs), distributors, and wholesalers. This definition is different than promotional campaigns that work across selling channels, like direct mail, email blasts, and online selling, which is more accurately termed "channel *marketing*".

I'll be guiding you through a process that will deliver greater results for the cooperating partners. You'll learn the pros and cons of various promotional opportunities and how to determine the best combination to meet the needs and buying behaviors of your target market segment. You'll also discover some effective ways to incorporate the promotions component into your program for channel partners and how those promotions will help to increase recognition for your product or service and continue to build your brand.

You'll learn how to brainstorm the promotional idea, plan for a successful campaign, execute it, and measure the results. Step by step, I'll show you the do's and the don'ts to help you sidestep the pitfalls that befall the lesser learned channel marketers.

Throughout the book, we'll focus on the purpose of your promotions and why you must set measurable goals for each one right from the beginning in order to evaluate its success. What's the objective of your promotion? Are you trying to increase sales? Raise brand awareness? Sell a slow-moving product versus a new one? Manage the life-cycle of an older product by reducing price through an "instant rebate" prior to a permanent price drop?

After you've decided the channel promotion is your new route for success, let's figure out how to craft and implement a great one. How can you team with another channel partner for your promotion? Will it fit your brand, your target audience? Or, as you roll out your promotion, does it sound creative but spark some nagging doubts about the results you can expect? We'll look at ways to create successful calls to action that drive the end-user to purchase *your* product rather than the one perched next to it on the shelf. Of course, you'll need to make sure you have ways to measure your promotion's results so that you can either forge ahead or regroup and adjust a few things. And I'll offer you a quick hit list of things to consider when planning your promotion.

Now what if, after all this careful planning and strategizing, your promotion flops? Did you think the promotion through enough? Was the message muddled? Did it appeal to your target audience or did you miss the mark? Keep in mind, not every promotion is successful, not even the best-planned campaigns. Some of the greatest successes were borne of failures! We'll talk about ways to regroup, redesign, and "re-promote" so you hit the mark the next time around — and to give you some checkpoints to avoid those pitfalls altogether!

And lastly, we'll explore the all-important results measurement. Every promotion must be measurable. You'll be investing a lot of your time and resources into creating a promotion, and you must be able to accurately measure those efforts in order to determine whether or not to run the promotion again in the future, to retool it, or to simply toss the idea in the circular file. We don't call this "trial and error". More accurately, it's a process of discovery!

Studies prove that an integrated promotion that works over multiple sales channels delivers stronger results — higher click-through rate, more sales — and a customer who purchases across several channels spends more money and maintains greater loyalty. So, it logically follows that a promotion involving the efforts of more than one channel partner will give you a distinct advantage.

The only question that remains is, what are you waiting for? Grab your partners and tune into the power of channel promotions!

Chapter 1

The Channel Promotions Line-up

So, what the heck is a "channel promotion"? And why should you even care about learning more? "Sounds like extra work and very complicated." Well, you've come this far in the book, so I've got to believe you have the interest and desire to use channel promotions to grow your business.

Here's what this strategy is all about. You have an absolutely killer product that you've been developing, and now you need to turn to your channel partners and end users and convince them your new product is their best purchase choice. You believe strongly in what you're selling but you need to motivate them to try something new. Ask yourself this: Why should they do that? Why should they abandon their comfort zone with the product they've been using (or selling) and give your newbie a try? Before you choose your channel promotion, you need to understand how to position the product so that you score a direct hit on that touchpoint in your consumer, whether that is the channel partner or the end-user.

Simply shouting superlatives about your great, new idea won't work because all manufacturers believe their products are the best! Fixing your product's price point at a very competitive rate is one way, but that dead-end route quickly can take you down the path of setting too low of a price and ruining your margins. Remember, once you've dropped your street price, there's no going back!

Implementing a program of channel promotions offers a way for you to get channel partners and their sales force to focus on pushing your product (versus the competition's) through incentives. At the end of the day, you are providing those partners with a series of promotional programs that will help them go to market and directly to the end-user with your products. These promotions and incentives may benefit the sales person, the channel partner or the end-user — or all three!

Push Me, Pull You

Your job is to push "selling solutions" for a specific audience — the three mentioned above (sales person, channel partner, end-user). This is not a one-promo-fits-all fix. What might work for the channel partner in a storefront or online may not help an outside sales force. And just because a channel partner believes you have a great promotion does not equate to a sense of urgency for the end-user to buy. How do you keep all the links in the chain functioning?

The push-pull strategy is the approach that has proven to be most effective. You push your sales channel by equipping them with the promotional arsenal they need to effectively sell your product to the end-user AND motivates them to, in turn, push really hard for results. This weaponry needs to include enthusiasm! We all know that an energized salesperson is a successful one. So you excite the reseller with incentives that will motivate this partner to put your product out there prominently in the face of the end-user.

The "pull" side of this strategy requires temptation. You need to entice the end-user to go looking for your product. This goes back to my earlier question: Why should they buy your product? What tempting offer can you dangle that will lure them into the waiting arms of the reseller?

The beauty of this push-pull approach is that it can liven up the sluggish channel partner, particularly if this channel partner sees the flurry of interest prompted by your promotional efforts to the end-user. As part of your incentive to the channel partner, you advise them that you are making the effort to drive traffic their way. This is a big plus in any channel partner's book. "You're going to bring me leads? Hey, I'm in!"

Choose Your Channel

By helping channel partners go to market with your brand, you establish a platform that generates success, not only for your product, but for the channel partner as well. There are various ways to make this work.

Let's take a look at some examples of the most common channel promotions and how and why they might work for you. Many of these promotions will work in tandem, offering your channel partners an easy and successful way to sell your products.

- o **Rebates.** We all know how rebates work, but the key is to keep the timeframe short. Allowing the customer to cash in on a rebate over the course of a long period of time sends the message that this "reduced pricing" may, in fact, become permanent. The long term doesn't provide the urgency needed to make the rebate successful. Mail-in rebates work well, especially for amounts less than $30 where you may get up to a 15% redemption (also known as "breakage") rate **and** capture great customer information for your database at the same time (love that win-win!). And while mail-in rebates do have an impact on every sale, you won't experience as much breakage as an in-store, instant rebate where everyone has the ability to cash in without providing the additional stats you deserve for your generosity. Instant rebates usually prompt a greater boost in sales because the end-user doesn't have to make any additional effort. It is, in effect, a price reduction. Before choosing one over the other, determine your ultimate goal: quick sales or more marketing data.

- o **POS Displays.** Point-of-sale displays are found at check-out counters, cash registers, or any place where a sales transaction can take place. The goal is most often to grab the impulse buy, capturing the attention of the customer who is killing time, waiting in line. And while the POS display promotes your product, typically, it is placed at a distance from where your products are merchandised and therefore are very difficult to track your return on investment (ROI). Be wary when a channel partner asks you to buy-in to their POS program as it will be very difficult to track this promotion's results.

o **Spiffs.** The Sales Program Incentive Fund delivers an added incentive to a channel partner's sales staff to drive greater sales of your product or line. For a new product, spiffs definitely grab the attention of sales reps! Who doesn't like earning a bonus? And you can tailor it in many ways — cash rewards, gift cards, free product, and travel opportunities. The benefits are short-lived, however: take away the spiff and you remove the incentive for selling more product for you. Some channel partners won't allow monetary spiffs, so make sure you inquire about guidelines; if they don't, you can still offer other incentives, like give-away merchandise including t-shirts, products, and software, instead of cash.

o **Buy-Get.** We constantly see these promotions in stores – Buy One, Get One (Buy-Get). It could be buy one, get one free; buy one, get one 50% off, buy 3, get 1 free … whatever you choose to offer as a promotion to your channel partners. Be sure to work with your channel partners to determine ways to track these promotions so you don't end up "giving away the store." This offer requires careful planning and execution to ensure you don't accidentally create a gray market for your product where your free "Get" is resold. Many "free" or reduced price bonus items or bundled components end up on eBay and not only hinder future sales but can also weaken your brand credibility.

o **Co-op Advertising**. While print and broadcast ads can be extremely expensive and the results are even harder to track, co-op advertising offers a way for you to encourage channel partners to run an ad or utilize a co-marketing campaign that showcases your products and reflects your brand. Your resellers earn co-op dollars through their product purchases from you to pay for part of the ad placement or co-marketing campaign. The more they buy from you, the more cash incentive they get, in the form of advertising monies. You create and place the ads, produce the mailing, or do the telemarketing, providing quality control and ensuring that your products are the only featured brand. Build an incentive or promotion to track in the campaign so you have a way of measuring the campaign's success.

o **Bundling**. This promotion presents a great way to get under-selling products into the hands of end-users who haven't yet embraced it. Take a good seller and bundle it with your sluggish seller for a special price. People who are already interested in the "hot product" will likely be tempted to pay a bit more to get the add-on. And, if this bonus offer stimulates interest in your other product, you've built a stronger platform on which to lift it up.

o **Buying Allowance**. How can you upsell your channel partner? Offer a short-term volume discount to stimulate sales. The more they buy, the better the discount. The buying allowance can be particularly appealing to purchasing agents whose primary objective it is to save money for their employer!

o **Loyalty Programs.** With globalization creating so many options for buying, your success relies on the quality of your relationships. Building loyalty with any consumer — channel partner or end-user — is key to engaging them in a long-term relationship with you. Ultimately, this effort will help you build your brand and your sales. Instead of blasting communications and promotional opportunities to a large group of people who may or may not care about your products or services, connect one-on-one with your best customers and create individual programs that mutually benefit you both. Create a rewards structure that delivers bonuses such as cash back or free products when they reach specified levels. Develop offers and services that meet the specific needs of your target audience. A well-structured loyalty program puts you ahead of your competitors as the buyer has a solid reason to remain loyal to you. You'll build customer and channel partner loyalty and gain respect from them in that you have creative a program specific to *their* needs.

o **Giveaways**. Simple giveaways are a great way to give your channel partners a value-added promotion to increase the incentive for the parter to sell your product before your competitors'. Everyone loves getting something for free. Do you have a flash drive you can give away free with the purchase of a piece of software? Think of minimal cost possibilities that add value to your product and make it easier for your channel partners to sell. And, like the rebate program, you can ask them to register online and provide basic information in order to receive their "prize".

o **End caps.** An end cap is just what it sounds like – a large display at the end of a store aisle or other prominent retail space. Valued for their high traffic location, these end caps showcase your product, "pull it away" from the competition in the traditional middle-of-the-aisle placement, and increase your sales of that product. Such perceived premium placement comes with a cost, of course. Space in a retailer setting is real estate, and the end caps are prime. More often than not, the increase in sales doesn't justify the high cost of an end cap. If you do pursue this route, make sure you request that your channel partner place *some* of your product – not all –at the end of the aisle. You should still keep a supply mixed in with the competition's offerings in the traditional middle location. If not, your product could easily be perceived as out-of-stock and a customer will by a competitor's product because yours isn't staring them in the face in the spot they expect to find it.

o **Staff Training**. If your channel partner's sales reps know the ins and outs of your product and you provide easy ways and promotions for them to sell it, you all benefit. By giving them the tools they need to effectively sell your product, you provide them the opportunity to cash in on greater sales and, in turn, generate more orders for you! Offer your channel partners on-site staff training where you can give them in-depth information about your product. Then offer them an incentive to buy the product at a reduced price (a product demonstration unit). Remember: Sales people sell what they use. If they're using your product, they're more likely to sell that, versus a competitor's. In your hands-on training session, point out the unique features that will make the selling process easier for them. Make sure they test it out and get comfortable with it. Your job is to spark their excitement. Be sure to show them the obvious and the obscure benefits. Teach them shortcuts and the value-added features. Get them to fall in love with your product and your company. If the reseller's sales staff knows you are working together as a team, they will be more motivated to sell your products over those from a vendor who doesn't give them the time of day.

Ultimately, channel promotions deliver ways to offer your channel partners the knowledge, incentive, and tools they need to aggressively sell your product ahead of the less supportive and appealing competition's. If you effectively equip them, you'll be well on your way to successfully selling through in no time!

Chapter 2

Promotions With a Purpose

Now that you have an idea about the different types of channel promotions that you can create, we have to define the purpose for you to even consider implementing these campaigns. Remember, all of your promotions must be measurable! For that to happen, you need a clear purpose – or goal – of what you want to accomplish. What measuring stick will you use to evaluate the success? Gear your promotions around achieving your goals, whether it's to increase incremental sales, improve customer satisfaction, build your brand, training, or to move "old" product.

Keep in mind, that channel promotions are typically short-term events designed to reward channel partners. Think of your promotions as energetic bursts of marketing

What's Your Objective?

Promotions work when you pinpoint the objective and tailor your channel promotion to drive the results that are required to meet your goal. First, let's look at your "big picture" and determine that objective. There are many reasons to execute a promotion. Here are the most common ones:

- Build brand recognition

- Offer direct sampling or buy-in opportunities at a reduced rate

- Create a short-term sales boost

- Sell slow-moving product, either individually or through bundling

- Drive traffic to your website

- Generate new sales leads or to get more business from your existing customers by cross-selling and up-selling

Sure, all of these goals sound tempting, don't they? And, while a carefully crafted channel promotion can deliver on more than one result, don't try to tackle all of these objectives with one idea. I guarantee that you will not get the same degree of success as if you focused your attention on one or two goals. Zoom in on your most pressing concern and build your promotion to hit it square on the head!

Let's say you need to create a channel promotion that "sells" the value of a partnership with you. Where do you start? Take a mental inventory of the benefits and successes a new channel partner should expect by developing a relationship with you. Then, focus on creating a channel promotion around your specialty product training, which will help to position you as the leader and resource of a particular product. Consider a promotion to offer product training for a new partner in order to empower them to sell-through to the end user with ease. You offer your new partner a toolbox of insider tips and ease-of use ideas – a complete, turnkey support system taught through your training program. As part of the promotion, offer an incentive to buy the product at a reduced price so that can know what they're selling inside and out. As I said earlier, what they know, they will sell. In turn, this not only benefits their bottom line, but yours as well, and positions your brand as the "go-to" and best source for product training.

Next, integrate the end-user into this promotional strategy. You offer a free demo package or bundle via a coupon that is redeemable at an authorized dealer — which is, you guessed it, the channel partners who have undergone the training! So, you reward their investment in building their product knowledge by driving customers to them. These channel partners then recognize that you strongly support their success, thus boosting your spot on their loyalty meter.

Whatever your objective, your promotion must include a total turnkey system

for selling through to the customer, whether that's the channel partner or the end user. Make it a no-brainer. Don't expect them to contribute more time and money to make it all happen, because your promotion will fail. Look at it like this: If someone asks you to join a committee and help achieve the group's mission, you're probably thinking, "how much time will this take?" However, if that same committee recruiter said, instead, "We need you to show up at our fundraiser and greet the guests for two hours", you'd probably realize that you have everything to gain, right? Organize the party and let your channel partners "just show up". Make them look great and you, in turn, look spectacular in their eyes.

Treat your channel partners well and provide them great service just as you would to your best customers. In your promotions, equip them with the necessary tools and materials to support the promotion, whether it's marketing materials, training the sales reps, providing simple giveaways like tee shirts or coffee mugs, or spiffs. If you do this each time as part of your "promotions with a purpose" checklist, you'll not only set the goal for that particular promotion, you'll also continue to build your brand as the Super Vendor, which, in conjunction with its primary purpose, every channel promotion should do.

Chapter 3

Crafting the Ultimate Promotion

Let's look at how you can tackle a sales challenge by applying channel promotions. You've determined that you need to stimulate sales. So, you look at your reports and identify the slow-movers. Where are they in their product lifecycle? Have they matured? Did they never actually realize their potential? Let's narrow the target down to one that has the most unrealized potential.

What do you think is the source for this lack of performance? Is it priced correctly? How have your competitors priced comparable products?

Now ask yourself if the market has not fully appreciated the value of this product. Unless you've got a dud or an overpriced item on your hands, this is likely the case.

Next, complete this sentence: This product would sell better if only
_____.

Here are some possible answers that can be addressed with channel promotions:

(a) the end-users understood what it can really do for them.

(b) my channel partners would make the effort to push it to the end-users.

(c) I could get it in the hands of the end-users to try it out.

Let's tackle the solutions one at a time.

(a). The end-users don't understand what your product can really do for them.

This is an awareness/understanding issue. If your product isn't easy to sell just from the information on the package, then you have to rely on your channel partner to make an extra effort. At the same time, you may need to revamp the packaging. Add a sticker with simple benefit statements, like "Faster Than XYZ", "Rated Best Value" or "The Ultimate Time Saver". Your goal is to educate the end-user and motivate the channel partner. So, here's your channel promotions solution:

- Implement a training program to excite and educate the sales staff.

- Offer SPIFFs to *really* motivate the sales staff.

- Bundle the product with a stronger seller and price the combined package at the retail cost of the strong seller, and add a cost-plus-10 margin on the targeted slow-mover.

- Send an e-blast to introduce the promotional plan to your channel partners.

- Produce a separate e-blast that you can send to the database of participating partners.

- Go back to the customers enrolled in your loyalty program and offer the product as a reward (either free with other purchase or at a reduced price)

- Create point-of-sale materials to promote the bundle.

(b) My channel partners are not making the effort to push my product to the end-users.

Your slow mover has potential but it doesn't have the ability to sell itself. So, it's sitting on a shelf because the channel partner is too busy selling other products. It's not a new product but probably never got the attention it needed to prosper. Think of this one like the runt of the litter. Just give it a little extra attention, in the form of a channel promotion campaign:

- Start with a SPIFF to get the attention of your channel partner's sales force.

- Also offer the product for free or at a deep discount to the sales team so that they can try it out and fall in love with it.

- Launch a training program that zeroes in on hitting the end-user's touchpoints.

- Offer an instant rebate.

- Create a POS display, perhaps a simple self-talker to bring attention to the product and the rebate offer.

- Blast the channel partners with an email campaign. Create a landing page on your site that features the promotional information. You might even consider testing two different offers and segmenting your list to see if there is a difference in the response rate.

(c) End-users need to sample the product to fully appreciate its value.

Seeing is believing. One taste and you're sold. Try it, you'll like it. These clichés refer to the undeniable fact that some products need to be sampled before they can be sold. That's why automobile dealers encourage the test drive. Once you inhale that new car smell, you're halfway sold. Hit the accelerator and you're closing in on making the deal. So, how do you execute a test-drive promotion that will rev up your sales?

- Plan a Demo Day or a risk-free offer to the end-user (e.g., money-back guarantee, free return shipping).

- Invest in exhibit space at a trade show where buyers can get a hands-on test run.

- Either bundle the product with a strong seller or do a Buy-Get where the "Get" is the slow mover.

- Offer a SPIFF to the sales staff that rewards them for their volume of "test drives" for the product.

- Sponsor a contest where "test drivers" are automatically entered to win prizes.

- Join forces with an affiliate partner that sells non-competitive products or services to the same market as yours. Bundle your product with theirs to reach a potentially untouched portion of your market segment.

These are just a few examples. You need to tailor your channel promotions plan to the challenges and benefits of your product, the type of sales channels you're using, and the needs, interests, and buying behaviors of your end-users. To make the planning a little easier, here is your step-by-step checklist for building channel promotions program.

1. **Come up with a killer idea**. Aim for something that's going to grab the end-user's attention or at least provide your channel partners with the means to do so. What might make your promotion an irresistible attention-grabber? What would excite this audience? Remember that in a multi-channel world, the needs of one audience (e.g., your channel partners) might not match those of another (e.g., end-user). Determine what your channel partners and/or end-users need that they're not getting from anyone else and then capitalize on that.

2. **Choose the appropriate promotions**. Turn back to chapter one and review some of the different channel promotions and then determine which combination will fit best for your target audience. Create an end-user promo, like a buy-get bundle or instant rebate, to draw customers into the store. Or do a drawing for an iTouch or high-def television to

draw customers AND capture names for the channel partner's database (and yours). Then set up a spiff that rewards salespeople who can up-sell these customers and supply them with promotional items like t-shirts and cd cases with your logo. Create a competition among the staff with some great prizes for top sales efforts. By simply evaluating each promotion's reach and potential, you can tailor a program specific to your partner or end-user.

3. **Will it work?** Now comes the hard part: trying to decide whether or not the promotion will actually deliver the results you expect. Does the theme fit with your brand? Will it appeal to your target audience? How does it work with the desired objective (remember, we talked about making sure you knew your goal and objective back in Chapter 2)? Let's say your creative team comes together and develops this unbelievable promotion designed to boost sales for a product that has under-performed. Your idea is to deliver an actual toolbox to your channel partners, filled with clever marketing tools and campaign elements that relate to the whole "tool" theme. Your creative team has found actual toolboxes, designed marketing collateral and supporting materials for the sluggish product, and you're ready to ship the box to your partners. "Hammer out the kinks in your sales slump." "Nail down the big sale." "Don't get screwed by bad service." It sounds perfect to you. The problem is, you've been creative in developing your promotion simply for the sake of being creative. Big mistake. You lost sight of your goal of bringing attention to this under-valued product. Chances are, if you have a product that has poor sell-through, it may need a promotion that addresses its price point or significant benefits (that are obviously not being embraced by the market) versus something with a lot of flash that doesn't zero in on the fundamental problem. A low price point or bundling will probably have better success here.

4. **Buy Me! Buy Me!** What's your call to action on this promotion you're considering? Make sure you clearly communicate to your customers what

you want them to do. Don't ever assume a prospect instinctively knows what you want them to do. Dropping the price may encourage end-users to buy but you then need to make it incredibly easy for them to make the purchase. Offering a spiff may provide an incentive to your channel partner's sales force to sell your product versus the competition's but you need to be clear about **how** they should effectively sell your product. If your message is muddled, your channel promotion will flop because what you've done is set up a scenario that excites the end-user but you then turned and walked away, feeling confident that they certainly know how to take it from there. Develop a call to action that will effectively drive the response that you want, and keep it simple with one or two ideas.

5. **Timing is everything.** Part of the planning process for a successful promotion is the schedule. Establish your goal for launching the promotion. Work backwards to create a timeline that puts every step in place so you can meet that schedule. You might also be tempted to roll out a promotion to stimulate sales during a dry period, like the first quarter drought. You need to be aware of the mindset of your market at this point so you can target a promotion that will motivate them to buy. "Start the new year with a resolution to succeed. Here's how." Think about the needs, desires, and motivation of your target audience and then craft the promotion around them. As I mentioned in the last point, being creative for the sake of being creative will lead to failure.

6. **Provide support.** Your promotional checklist should include all the ways that you can offer support of this promotion. Go for the co-op advertising dollars we talked about in Chapter 1 or create a direct mail or email campaign. The more ways you are able to offer support to a particular promotion, the more buy-in you'll have from your channel partners – or you'll have purchases from your end-users. Map out a strategy for the idea and think through the entire promotion from start to finish. Examine every step. How will it work and what will it need for support through each stage?

Will you need postcards to jumpstart interest? What items do you want to include as spiffs and where will you get them? How about special packaging for bundling? You're now taking that killer promotional idea and filtering it out so it works. And don't forget to look to your channel partners, too, to see what resources they can provide. For example, do they have specific customer lists that are prequalified for this particular product? Offer to mail to those lists on their behalf. Map out your plan, step by step, and you create a blueprint for a rock-solid promotion.

7. **Did it work?** Lastly, but most importantly, you must have a way to measure your promotion. We've already started talking about this in the book, and we'll talk about it more in-depth in Chapter 5, but whatever you do, make sure you create a promotion that will generate trackable results and allow you to evaluate the promotion's success or failure. Then look at those results and evaluate your efforts. But that's for another chapter....

By using these simple guidelines and checklist, you can create your own plan for each promotion, which will help you stay on track and think about all the aspects you need to consider when planning a promotion. Crafting a great promotion is like making a great cake from scratch. You're blending all the original, simple ingredients to create something that tastes so good!

Chapter 4

When a Good Idea Goes Bad

Armed with your newfound knowledge, you're about to set off to create the slam-dunk promotion that takes off with wings. But failure can happen. What do you do if it does? How do you regroup and get back on track in a positive direction? Better yet, how do you avoid future flops?

In this chapter, I'll help you learn from mistakes, with the goal of avoiding them altogether. We'll wander through the common pitfalls so you can sidestep them in your planning and execution of channel promotions.

Before we move on to perusing the biggest flop factors, let me just say that, if your promotion does fail, I applaud you. Yes, bravo! A failed promotion probably means that you pushed your limits and were trying to succeed at something that was at the threshold of being beyond your limits. If you only attempt things that you know how to do, and don't step outside your comfort zone when it comes to marketing, then, chances are, not only is your channel promotion going to fail, but your big picture business model will crumble as well. If you're taking on challenges and creating new promotions that stretch your capabilities, then you are headed for success. Dr. Linus Pauling, a brilliant scientist, said, "The way to get good ideas is to get lots of ideas and throw the bad ones away." So keep coming up with ideas, lots of them, and let's look at how you can filter the good ideas from the bad ones.

The Top Three Flop Factors

Sometimes, the answer to finding the cause of a failure is easy. The price was too high — or too low (the consumer thought it had no value). The timing was off. The execution was sloppy. Or the idea was just plain rotten.

Let's take a look at the most common causes of a failed promotion.

#1. Band-Aids Cover, They Don't Fix

We've already talked about this in earlier chapters, but the key to executing any great channel promotion is in the planning. Careful planning puts you on the path to success. Flying by the seat of your pants does not. It just leaves your butt exposed!

So what happened? Did you fall in love with the anticipated outcome and, in your passionate zeal, forget to follow through on essential details? Did you have a creative idea for your channel partners that presumed they would buy into a bundle, only to be hit with indifference? Did you create a rebate or buy-get offer that sold hundreds of widgets but actually *cost* you money in sales versus unloading old inventory? And keep in mind even the best-intentioned, well thought-out promotion can flop instead of having people flip.

I recently spoke with a marketing person who was desperate to placate her resellers, who were complaining about price points. That was their excuse for not selling the product. Rather than explore the reason for the sluggish sales, she hastily dropped the price. The channel partner then dropped the price a hair, but took advantage of the price cut to boost her margin. While the vendor saw a brief rise in sales, they lost their margin and lowered the street price of a product that was actually priced fairly to begin with.

The real problem here was not price, but lack of training. The sales staff did not adequately understand the product's features and, therefore, could not convey its added value to the end-user so sales were down. Why spend 25% more for something if you think you can get the same features in a lesser-priced version? I don't fault the end-users for being frugal because they had no reason to spend more. And I don't blame the channel partner for seizing an opportunity to grab greater margins without making any more effort. The fault lies in the marketer's priorities. She chose to calm the angry dogs, so she threw them a bone rather than train them to behave appropriately. Maybe there should be a new job function in the corporate world: Sales Whisperer!

Look at your idea from the perspective of the recipients. If you can't do that, pass it around to people you know, preferably those who match the demographic profile of your intended audience. Ask them how they would react to this concept. What message does it send? What does it say about the company sending it? What questions does it leave you with? Do a focus group with a select group of customers before you launch the promotion, if you're unsure.

And, most of all, before you jump into a promotion, be clear about what you expect to gain. Determine, specifically, how this idea will meet that objective,

#2. Pass the Cheese, Please.

So you've created this amazing promotion that you believe the channel partners' sales teams are going to embrace wholeheartedly. It's a no-brainer. You've got a spiff that will reward your high-performing sellers with free products and cash bonuses. And a rock-solid promise to the consumer, along with a mail-in rebate. Your idea is clever—so clever that you risk dislocating your shoulder by patting yourself on the back. You're going to tell the world that you're so confident this particular widget will make their lives easier, that you'll give them the shirt off your back if it doesn't. You even convinced your CEO to pose, shirtless, in the photo for the promotional materials, so that the public can connect with him personally, like Dave Thomas and Frank Perdue.

You have all the pieces in place, how the promotion is going to work, what the sales force will need in order to execute it with their customers, and you're ready to present it to them. And you do. And there's complete silence from the crowd. Then some snickers (and not the edible kind). The marketers were counting on the kitchy appeal of their quirky concept. They counted wrong.

The promotion you thought was professional, creative, and a wonderful tool ready-made for the sales force, is, well, cheesy. The channel partners, who know their customers inside and out (and clearly you may not), are totally underwhelmed. While the spiff may *sound* generous, they know that their actual bonuses will be miniscule because customers are not going to race to the store to buy this software.

Look at the uproar of an advertisement featuring Spain's 2008 Olympic basketball team. The ad was to promote a courier company that sponsored the team. Every team member was paid to make "slant eyes" in the group photo. No one—not the players, coach, advertising agency, photographer, or anyone on the marketing team—saw a problem with this. Yet the ad ran right before the Olympics, which, by the way, were being held in *China*! And one of the other team sponsors is—or should I say, "was"—a Chinese-owned shoe company! One might ask, "What were they thinking?!" And you might answer, "They weren't."

So what do you do? First, recognize that not *all* of your promotion may be cheesy. But clearly you weren't tuning in to whom the sales force would be speaking. I cautioned you earlier to avoid being creative for the sake of being creative. Your first step should guide you to look this captive audience in the eye and ask them what parts of the promotion would work for them and what parts won't. Listen to them. Then gather up all of their suggestions and head back to the drawing board. Tweak what could work and ditch what won't. Show your channel partners that you're in this for the long haul and want to make sure the promotions you create for them to use will work for them successfully. If this means reworking the parameters of the promotion a few times, presenting it, and then honing it again, that's OK. With every extra step you take in the planning/tweaking/testing stage, you fine-tune the promotion and build its success rate.

#3. One Size Does *Not* Fit All.

A promotion that works for one target audience may not work for another, so there's a good chance that you developed a successful promotion, only to have it fail because it didn't appeal to the right audience. Mining your database and knowing the needs of your customers and channel partners will allow you to tailor promotions that zero in on a particular set of needs. Another good indication as to your promotion's potential for success is to determine whether or not it's a one hit wonder versus a long term friend. In other words, are you simply offering up the promotion to crank up sales for a particular product or drive more traffic to your website today? Are you creating the promotion to build your long-term reputable brand with these channel partners and end-users? These are all great reasons for launching a channel promotion, but each goal has its own set of needs. One promotion will not fit all. You may have some channel partners who need the one hit wonder here and now for sales purposes. That's fine for your goal of generating short-term revenue. But does it succeed in building lasting relationships? No. Price breaks never do.

One of the most important components in running a successful promotion is taking the time to pull back and analyze every step with an objective eye. You need to separate yourself from you, the seller, and step into the shoes of me, the buyer. Remember the almighty acronym of marketing success: WIIFM ("What's in it for me?").

For a channel promotion to succeed on all levels (distributor, reseller, retailer, end-user), you need to address the unique needs, their business models and desires of each channel. What will make each one respond in the way you want? Create a chart of those needs and compare them to each other. You'll find that what the end-user wants and needs rarely matches those of the distributor. So don't expect one single promotion to do the work of a smartly crafted channel promotion!

Ultimately, if your promotion tanks, there's a good reason. Take a deep breath and then really tune in on what *did* work and what *didn't*. Then revisit those parts that need some more refining. Go back to the drawing board. Listen to your channel partners and customers to what their needs are. Great channel promotions that are planned, tested, and tweaked will work. And the not-so-great-ones? Filter out the junk and see what remains, just like panning for gold. Shine it up and you could have a winner!

Chapter 5

Weighing the Cost, Measuring the Return

If you've gotten this far in the book, then you're probably wondering, "Well, what the heck is this all going to cost me?" And if you've read my book, "Great Marketing is Free," you'll know that there are various ways to skin that costly cat, so to speak.

Certainly, many channel promotions can be created and executed with little or no budget. But you must also weigh the cost-versus-return of doing a promotion for little or no money, some money, or a big budget. A great idea isn't truly great if the cost involved to execute it won't deliver the desired result. On the flip side, if you've mapped out a strategy at little or no cost, but your *time* involved to pull it off is astronomical, then where is the added value? How much is your time worth here? Could it be used for a better profit-maker than this particular promotion? If you're giving away product, selling at reduced prices for a bundle or special buy-get offer, what's the potential drag on future post-promotion sales?

These are all questions you must think about and answer carefully so that you don't waste precious money *or* time when you create channel promotions. Time *is* money! If you don't believe that, ask any service provider who gets paid by the hour.

The Napkin Lives!

If you know me or have read my articles and books, you already know that I love to use the Back-of-the-Napkin Model as an example of where your money might be spent, what kind of return you might get and whether or not the program is worth doing at all. This idea also ties back to the goal that every promotion that you create and execute should be measurable. By determining whether or not your promotion is cost-effective before you actually executive it can save you from one great big, costly headache.

So for the big picture and for those of you who aren't familiar with the Back-of-the- Napkin Model, let's take a look:

A. Cost to create and execute the promotion	$5,000
B. # of responses	2,500
C. Cost per response	$2.00 (A divided by B)
D. # who purchased	75
E. % who purchased	3% (D divided by B)
F. Cost per customer	$66.67 (A divided by D)

Armed with this type of data, whether it comes from previous promotions or a carefully estimated budget, you can determine whether or not the promotion might succeed or fail – *before* you put the wheels in motion. Will the cost per customer deliver a breakeven point for you? Are there other spiffs or incentives you might have to offer your channel partners' sales forces in order to get them to buy into your promotion?

Let's look at another example using co-op advertising. You're running an end-user rebate program for a new product and you're planning a combination of direct mail and email to registered users. You contact your channel partners and offer to put their contact information at the bottom of the marketing campaign material to drive local customers directly to them (dealer tags). You actually handle the printing, mailing, and emailing using their lists. All they have to do is agree to foot half the cost and you do the rest. A no-brainer for the channel partner, but does it make fiscal sense for you?

Go back to the back-of-the-napkin model and examine your expenses in doing this mailing. Look at the creative costs, plus the printing and postage. What is the size of the partners' lists? What can you expect for a response rate? How many of those can you expect to close? Can you track the results, traffic, inquiries, and/ or sales that you might get from this one particular mailing? Will the cost involved deliver your desired results? Maybe. Maybe not.

The same holds true for spiffs. While you may be ready to offer incentives to your sales force or your channel partners, weigh the cost of the reward you will give to the sales staff against the profit in the added volume from the sales they generate. Be careful not to cut too deeply into your potential profits. Think of creative ways to get buy-in on your product from the sales team without luring them with an overly generous spiff. Perhaps offer a deep discount on a piece of software you want them to sell for you. This is a win-win, because instead of laying out cash, you've put the product in the hands of a salesperson who can test it out and sell it with confidence. Of course, you might want to also consider a training session with each team to ensure they're opening that package. Again, map out your plan of attack prior to moving forward and weigh your options for the best – and most successful – channel promotions.

Summary

Channel promotions work. That's a fact. But they need the creativity, insight, and effort of the promoter. Somewhere between creating your product and making the sale is a wide chasm that needs to be bridged. You are trying to influence buyers, wherever they are in your chain. Your buyers are not merely the end-users. The channel partners who get your product into the hands of those end-users represent a target market that needs your attention. And, as we've learned, the needs of each group along the channel is distinctly different. So your message and the delivery model needs to be equally diverse.

A channel promotion is like the bridge you build across that great divide between product development and sales. Each piece of the promotional campaign brings you closer and closer to the desired result—whether that's greater brand recognition, fresh leads, a sales boost, or guiding the traffic across the bridge and to the threshold of your website. One step will not get you there. You can't just excite the reseller and walk away. Nor can you motivate the end-user without fueling the reseller with the tools he needs to close the deal. You must move your promotion from channel to channel or that bridge to your sales abruptly ends. You need to bring those channels together, meeting the needs and desires of each one, creating synchronicity that leads to sales.

In this book, we've covered the tools at your disposal and how to use them effectively. You've learned how to craft and execute the promotional idea. You know why and how to measure the success, and even how to pick yourself up when the results don't meet your goals.

Take a little time right now, while this information is still fresh, and give yourself the challenge to create a channel promotion. Before you do another thing, identify the channels in your chain. List the unique motivators that will influence each one to respond as you desire. Then use your newfound knowledge to connect them with the power of a channel promotion. Go forth and channel your brilliance!

ABOUT THE AUTHOR

A dedicated marketing professional, Michelle Kabele has been helping technology companies develop award-winning channel partner programs and marketing strategies for over 10 years. Her innovative channel marketing concepts have been adopted and implemented by many leading technology companies, including Zebra Technologies, 3Com Corporation, and U.S. Robotics. Moreover, Michelle has worked extensively with VARs throughout North America and thoroughly understands the realities and practicalities they face in planning and executing effective promotional, marketing, and sales campaigns.

Michelle has an MBA from the J.L. Kellogg Graduate School of Management (Evanston, IL) and an undergraduate degree from Northwestern University (Evanston, IL).

For more great ways to build your business, check out all of Michelle Kabele's books:

- *Great Marketing Is Free!*
- *All the Web's A Stage*
- *50 Smart, Easy and Effective Ideas to Boost Your Business Today*
- *Just Say Yes! The Power of Creative Thinking Way Outside the Tired Old Box*
- *The Pocket Guide to Marketing Speak: Stop Mouthing the Words and Start Using Them*

Visit www.ideastormpress.com for up-to-the-minute news, advice, ideas, and just cool stuff.

www.ingramcontent.com/pod-product-compliance
Lightning Source LLC
Chambersburg PA
CBHW070749210326
41520CB00016B/4646